New archaeological discoveries continue to push back the date of the first needles. The earliest were thought to be fish bones and once developed became one of the most efficient and unchanged tool in the history of the world. Metal needles date to at least 5th century BC (Mahenjo Daro, India). Blackthorns from the hedgerows were used quite effectively as early pins. (example below)

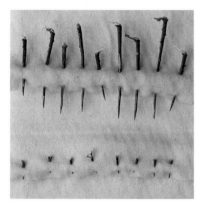

With needle, fibre and fabric so much is possible. We have rich cultural traditions to inspire us, although the organic nature of textiles means that very few ancient examples survive as they are subject to bacterial decay. Those that do survive have been preserved in unique conditions such as ice or airtight tombs. Although rare, their very fragility highlights the vulnerability of the makers. It is humbling to observe the wonderful textiles produced by people who had so little but achieved so much.
In many cases what was once an innovative response is now recognised as a tradition.

How can we use this information to develop fresh approaches to textiles? By challenging ourselves to reconsider working methods and materials, we may see beyond our comfort zone to rediscover the energy of invention. Inventiveness and resourcefulness is something we all have and we just need to tap into it to evince spontaneous and unusual solutions to tasks.

Challenge 1
Imagine being in an environment where the needle has not been invented and you need to join things together with only the most basic materials such as sticks, twigs, plant fibres and skins. How many different ways can be found of joining pieces together?

This has been a useful teaching exercise and the responses highly inventive, frequently developing into more resolved work. For experimental purposes students can use fabrics and threads as well as found objects but the challenge is the same.

Poking holes is often one of the first instincts and once holes have been made the possibilities are endless.
It might be helpful to work with strips of approximately 7cms-10cms and construct a sampler that can be used for future reference.

Among the basic methods possible the following can be achieved; binding, strapping, wrapping, knotting, tying (with or without bows), lacing, weaving, plaiting, toggles/primitive buttons using sticks or fabric lumps and skewers or stick pins.

These primitive constructions form the basis of most of our fastenings today. Forged of necessity they have been refined into an amazing array of functional and decorative forms. The sample pictured right shows some of the ways in which these primitive joinings could be made. This exercise could be further developed into three dimensional forms.

For inspiration we need to look no further than the nests in our gardens to see the ingenuity and skill of birds who construct their intricate structures using twigs and assorted plant materials.

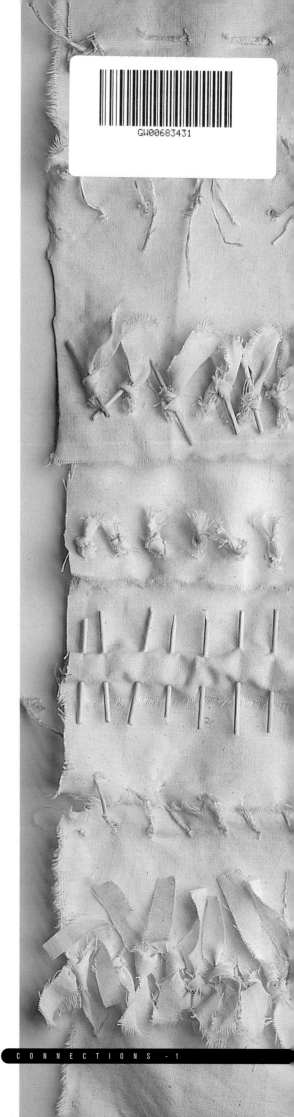

Having established the basic methods of joining pieces together, each one could be exploited and further developed into other work.

Many people have a haberdashery box, perhaps inherited, containing buttons, fastenings, press studs, hooks and eyes and even suspenders etc. These items are not just functional as they have historical resonance and can be used to establish context.

There are other domestic materials that can be used to link and join materials.

In the kitchen, cocktail sticks and skewers, freezer tags, clips and pegs, paper clips and treasury tags could all be employed to good effect.

The garden can also be full of innovative methods of joining things together. Plant ties, netting, clips, bean supports, fruit cages, bean poles, trellis and other support constructions can be an inspiration when researching joins.

Challenge 2
Selecting from a bank of fastenings, continue to join strips together using any items that you have and this time a needle and thread may be used.
Use conventional and unconventional fastenings for this purpose.

This is a limitless exercise so select those items that really appeal.

Right: *Using well washed, recycled cotton shirt fabrics, this sampler indicates some conventional and less conventional methods of joining two edges. There are hundreds of combinations and as well as an indicator of techniques such samplers could be developed into more resolved pieces.*

Lacing

Each aspect of joining and fastening materials together can become a specialised study and lacing has an extensive and varied history.
Sails have been lashed together and continue to employ lacing. Similar techniques are employed with tents and marquees so there is great strength when the holes are supported by metal eyelets.

It is perhaps in fashion that lacing has enjoyed it's most inventive and exotic variations. A study of laced corsets will reveal some of the fantastic decorative and highly technical constructions that have been used to shape, distort and punish the female form.

The technical details are fascinating and the social implications far reaching. Many textile artists refer to the information in their work.

Although there is great emphasis on visual research for textile artists, a study of historical aspects should not be underestimated as it can be fascinating and inspiring.
At a recent Vivian Westwood retrospective exhibition the importance of historical research was emphasised. Corsetry, lacing and distortion played an important part in influencing her highly innovative pieces.

Right: Two wall pieces by Anita Sturch exploit traditions of lacing and corsetry.

Although they are not functional they refer to traditional techniques and Anita has used personal and family references to inform her work.

Below: Sketchbook pages with observations based on corsets and historical examples of lacing along with technical experiments on different lacing configurations.

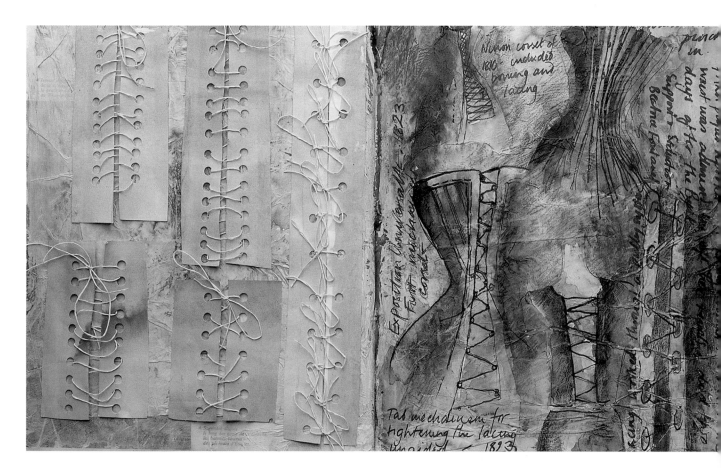

In Context

There are banks of knowledge that are generation specific and the use of textile techniques is one area that can really identify us. Coming from a generation that was taught needlework techniques and practical items as part of the school curriculum, most contemporaries would be certain to have that knowledge. The school cookery apron was a required element of needlecraft. Often detested at the time it can now be looked upon with a fond detachment. Most people were able to make some items of clothing although not everyone enjoyed it.

Paper patterns have a particular resonance and contain strong almost iconic graphics that have been incorporated by a number of textile artists.

Essential knowledge was considered to be the appropriate use of seams. These were first practised before their application in practical, if often unworn, garments.

Seams

Seam - *line of junction between two edges especially those of two pieces of cloth.*

The types of seam used have changed and developed over centuries. The use of a particular seam could indicate a period, conjure up a memory or establish historic resonance so it is useful to know a range as an addition to our technical reference.

If you see a bed sheet that has a seam down the middle it immediately establishes it as part of a time in the early to mid twentieth century when thrift and 'make do and mend' was encouraged. 'Sides to Middle' referred to the practice of prolonging the life of a worn bed sheet by cutting it in half and rejoining it with the side edges to the middle.

There are of course reference books but before looking them up it is interesting to see if by digging deep into the memory banks or being inventive, how many seams are possible.

> **Challenge 3**
> Make a strip sampler using as many seams as possible from memory. Hand and machine stitching could be included for this challenge.

There are many types of seam and they all have a specific purpose but they could be used decoratively for historical accent or decorative purposes.

Simple landscapes could be described using combinations of simple seams.

The decorative open seam has a long and honourable history and there are many specific and complex stitches that fill the gap between two edges of cloth efficiently and beautifully.

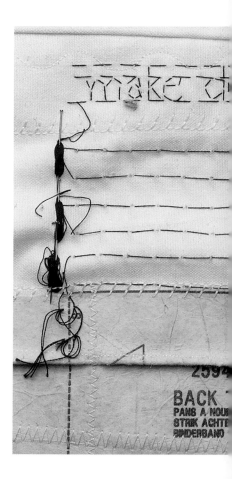

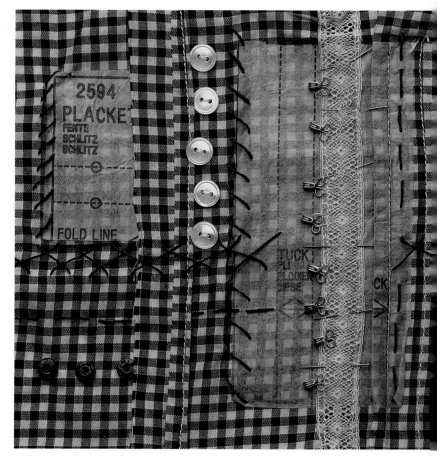

Right: This third strip sampler exploits a range of conventional seams including 'French', 'lap', 'run & fell' and 'decorative open seam'.

Left & Below: These small pieces celebrate needlework traditions through the selective use of traditional materials, techniques and sewing notions.

Pattern pieces, pins, seams, patches and smocking gathers are among the elements that help to suggest a sense of period.

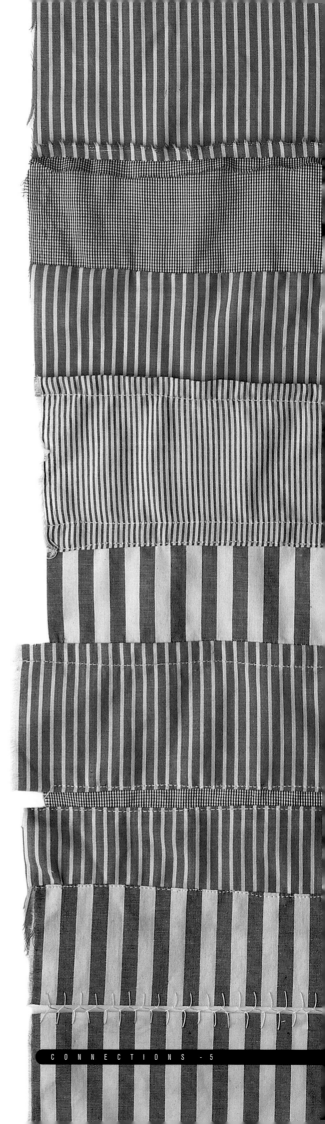

Decorative Open Seams

Traditionally, insertion stitches were used to create an open work decorative seam. Some books refer to the term 'faggoting' which is a name given to a number of stitches used within the technique.

Simple, attractive seams were made in the 16th century to join sleeves and yokes of shirts and other garments. Often worked on linen, in red or blue silk, many of the examples are illustrated in books or can be seen in museums. Throughout the ages beautifully executed examples have decorated babies gowns, lingerie and household linen. Some were so intricately worked they could look akin to lace. Other countries around the world such as Syria, Italy and Hungary have incorporated exquisite and colourful open seams on their embroideries.

Sadly over the years as with many traditional techniques, books and journals have sanitised this technique simplifying and presenting it in a bland way where colour and adornment was seldom considered.

The conventional method follows:
• Each of the two edges of fabric to be joined must be turned or rolled to form a narrow hem.

• The two edges should be carefully placed, pinned and tacked in parallel lines to a supporting material such as strong paper or card. The spacing between can vary from one to two centimetres depending on the selection of stitches.

• Remember to consider the purpose of the open seam. A decorative one would allow more freedom whereas practical issues would need to be considered if used within the construction of a garment. This would dictate the spacing, stitch and thickness of thread to ensure the required durability.

• A strong soluble stabiliser could be substituted for the card but only if the fabric and threads selected can withstand the washing away action.

• Ensure that the fabric is very firmly tacked to the support particularly the fastening on and off process so as to withstand the pull as the stitches are being formed.

• Work the stitches into the fabric only and NOT the supporting card with the exception of the soluble stabiliser.

• Traditional stitches include variations of buttonhole stitch and cretan stitch, which can be twisted, knotted or plaited.

• Keep the same 'pull' or tension through out the stitching process in order to keep an even space between the two edges.

• Experiment with other stitches not normally associated with this technique to experience their potential for holding the edge firmly for a strong as well as a decorative open seam.

• After some experimentation, ways of including or disguising stray linking threads and stabilising the main stitch will become obvious. The addition of contrasting, textured or coloured yarns or beads to adorn can also refine this action.

• In general, fasten the threads on and off within the crease of the hem or at the outer edges.

Although this technique may be considered as rather old fashioned, an unusual and attractive alternative can be created particularly if lateral thinking is applied. The fabulous

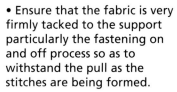

array of threads now available, partnered with a less conventional choice of stitch, could result in a fresh look for this ancient technique.

Open seams can be used to construct a garment, three-dimensional pieces, or be integrated within other works. Not only could they introduce a decorative element but alternatively fragmentation and reconstruction of certain imagery could be developed to have conceptual connotations.

Far Left: Sample showing a range of stitches worked on 'shot' synthetic taffeta: from the top, Cretan, sorbello, french knot, detached chain and raised chain band.

Left Centre: These unconventional samples show randomly placed felt shapes joined by blocks of straight stitches and partially worked detached chain stitches. Although not necessarily suitable for conventional usage, innovative joinings could be developed to use with panels, hangings and perhaps art wearables.

Above: Sorbello is the main stitch selected to be worked on Thai silk. Knots or beads have been incorporated alongside additional threads that wrap around and highlight parts of the stitch. The initial stitch worked on the wider band is Cretan with featherstitch worked on top. Metallised thread was wrapped around part of the base stitch. Partnered with appliqué, pin tucks or further beading, this technique could decorate a cuff of a jacket or be made into a richly patterned bag where the lining could show behind the open seams having been considered in the initial design.

Knots & Structures

Since the crucial discovery of knots as a method of fastening, people have been endlessly inventive in using them.

At their simplest they can hold together two or more items in a strong but utilitarian way. At their most elaborate they can be used in art and fashion in complex and decorative configurations. Tying shoelaces marks a significant point in a child's development.

Linked knots in various forms can be used to construct a range of fabrics from fisherman's nets to the finest laces.

Knotted cords formed a coded language in ancient Peru and knotted cords based on these traditional techniques are still popular today in the form of knotted 'friendship bracelets'.

Macrame is a complex structured discipline based entirely on knots.

The applications for the decorative, utilitarian and conceptual use of knots are so numerous that we can only touch on them here but experiments in this area will give spectacular starting points for both hand and machine.

There are some specific knotted fabrics that require specialised equipment such as the traditional knotted shuttle nets made by fishermen or 'lacis' nets that can be found with specialist suppliers. There are however many ways in which knotted fabrics can be fully exploited with basic equipment.

Using a simple wooden frame as a support it is possible to form a range of knotted fabrics under tension. The frame can be bound over with warp threads and weft threads knotted across in regular or irregular patterns.
After completion the knotted cloth may then be used as a base for hand or machine stitching which can add an interesting contrast to the more robust knotted fabric.
The knotted texture may be cut off the frame and utilised in a range of different ways.

The network can be supported on soluble fabric and machine stitching added as a contrast. If a solution of PVA glue is applied to the knotted cloth and allowed to dry, it will become a strong self supporting grid and this could prove useful for backgrounds.

Knots may be tied in fibres, cut up and applied to a background to achieve a highly textured fabric.

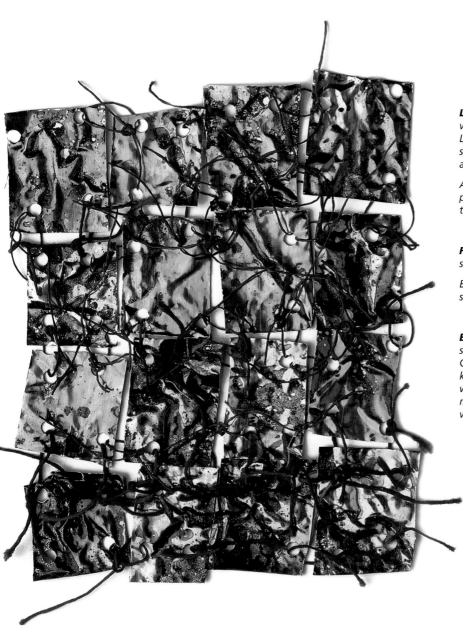

Left: *The metallic tiles used here were cut from tomato purée tubes. Lemon juice was painted on the surface before being heated to achieve a distressed look.*

A hole punch made the holes and paper fibre was used to tie the tiles together.

Far Left: *Paper fibre knotted grid strengthened with PVA glue.*

Beaded wires were then tied into the structure.

Below: *Sketchbook pages based on scaffolding patterns from Gaudi's Cathedral in Barcelona. Mixed media knot constructions using painted wooden skewers and paper fibre and mixed fibre knotted construction with bows at intersections.*

Knotting
& Knitting

There are examples of knots all around us.
The importance of this initially simple but versatile technique cannot be overstated.
The symbolic significance of the knot should not be overlooked.
The knot part of 'the noose' contrasts with the lovers' knot.
Knot gardens, 'tying the knot', 'tied to the apron strings', 'knotted up' and many others offer opportunities to use knot forms to express ideas.

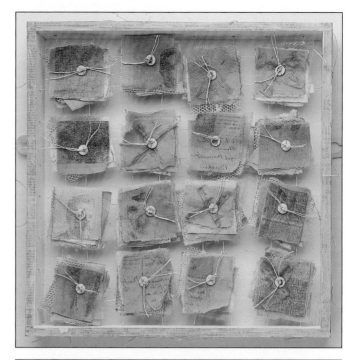

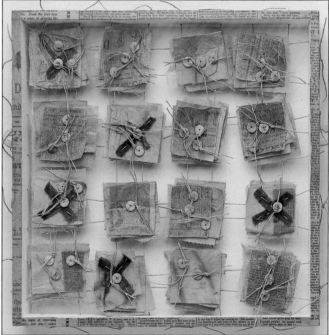

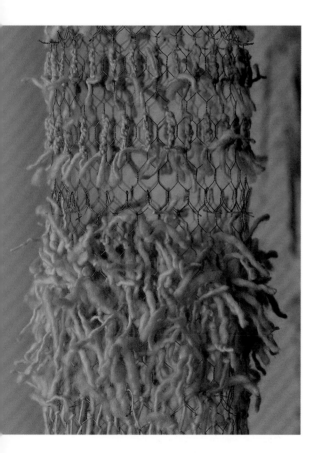

Above:
Mandy Scrivener worked this piece using a range of fibres on wire netting.

This was part of a series using knots as a vehicle for expressing personal ideas related to body forms.

Knitting can be very useful when progressing ideas particularly related to organic forms.

As a continuous loop technique it offers a rhythmic structure closely allied to the build up of cellular patterns in plants and mineral structures.

Good traditional knitters have been encouraged to keep even tension but uneven stitches and irregular knitting may offer the most interesting ideas.

Knitting may be used in combination with hand and machine embroidery and on water soluble material to create web like structures.

Once again experimental samples will help when exploring the range of possibilities.

Starting points could include:

• Fine threads on thick needles.

• Thick threads on uneven size needles.

• Vary fine and thick in the same piece.

• Try using paint brushes, twigs or wire as knitting needles. After all the first knitters had to improvise.

• Experiment with different threads including fine wires, paper fibre, torn fabric etc.

• Wind the yarn round the needle several times per stitch for large holes.

• Work stitches irregularly for organic effects.

• Overlay different scales of knitting for complex grids.

• Spray dye through the knitting onto a ground for a shadow effect.

• Knit in non dyed threads and dye afterwards.

• Tie the looped structures at the intersection to stabilise.

• Combine with paper pulp for intriguing textural effects.

• Suspend beads, fabrics or other materials onto the threads during the progress of the knitting.

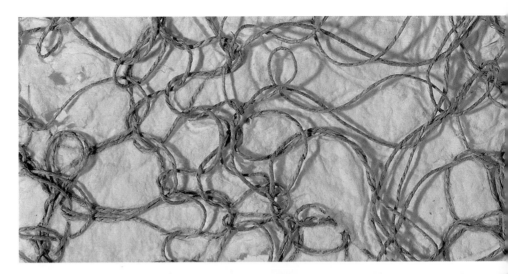

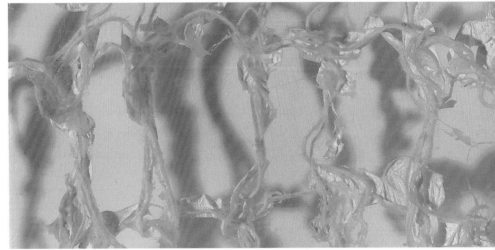

Left: These linked pieces use the device of knotted net structures to form the basis of work called 'Secrets and Lies'.

The three pieces 'White Lies', 'Blind Alleys' and 'Dark Secrets' exploit knots and refer to the way which we find out about our history.

Parchments, bundles of letters and papers and books reveal our past.

The more we learn the more we realise may lie uncovered. We are just touching on the mysteries of our past and new discoveries often give a lie to received wisdom, hence 'Blind Alleys'.

The form of the pieces also refers to the random nature of our knowledge.

We are totally dependant on chance discoveries so there are many 'Dark Secrets' to be uncovered.

Top: Open knitted linen structure placed on a jay cloth before wet paper pulp was pressed into it.

The knitting then became imbedded into the drying pulp.

As a variation to this, the knitting could be pressed into wet paper pulp and then removed to allow the structure to imprint.

Above: *This sample was worked using a combination of cotton fibre and 'Tyvek' cut into long strips.*

The two fibres were knitted very loosely on huge needles.

When complete the resulting structure was place between two sheets of baking parchment and a hot iron applied to 'melt' the structure into and organic form.

Further experiments could be made using varying fibres and thicknesses of 'Tyvek' for different effects.

These knitted structures were worked on huge needles.

1: 'Kunin' felt squares that had been distressed with a heat tool were suspended onto the copper wire before knitting. They were then knitted into stitches as required.

2: Knitted wire with additional net bows and fabric ties.

3: Cut plastic straws were knitted in a similar way onto beading wire.

4: To a base of open knitted net a layer of freely knitted textured yarn was connected with red safety pins.

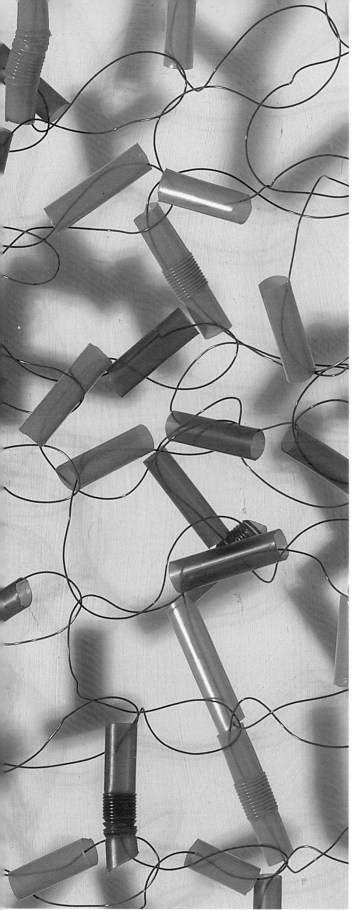

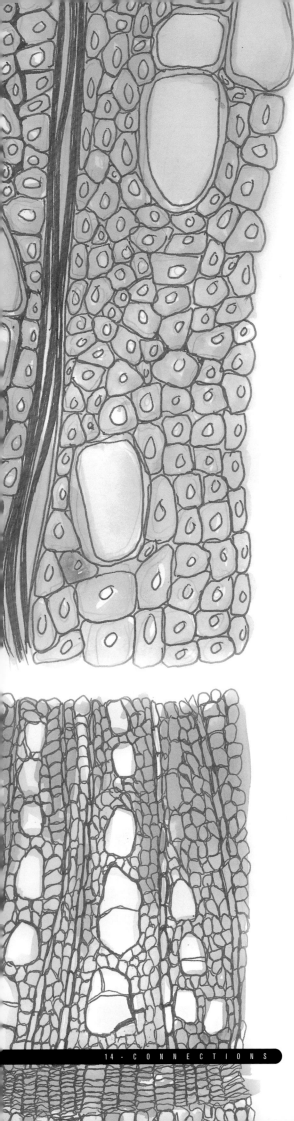

Organic Forms

Nature can provide us with all the inspiration we could ever need to exploit organic rhythms. Cells are linked to each other and expand and grow in logical progressions. The human body is full of linked networks and these are echoed in the natural forms supporting leaves, trees & plants. Microscopic examination reveals complex structures that may often be broken down to simple linked repeated units.

Patterns under the sea reflect the wave movements and so often resemble ever changing knitted structures. As a continuous loop technique, knitting grows from a stitch and builds up from a base line. It works well when influenced by organic forms in nature.

Left: *Two studies based in microscopic cellular patterns from trees. The linked structures have been used to inspire the knitted textures shown (right).*

Right: *The cellular pattern has been knitted on large needles using a linen thread. Once complete the structure was stretched on a wooden frame and dipped in paper pulp so that some of the pulp would adhere. The organic quality of the knitting dictates the rhythms of the piece. There is huge scope for development with these techniques.*

Top Right: *Open knitted sample structure using cotton yarn. When complete the knitting was supported on soluble paper before machine stitching anchored it down. This was worked in a frame. An interesting aspect of the paper soluble is that it will completely dissolve in water but an application of PVA or acrylic will act as a resist so that some of the paper ground can be preserved. In this case some coloured PVA was applied in areas, allowed to dry and then the remaining ground was dissolved in cold water.*

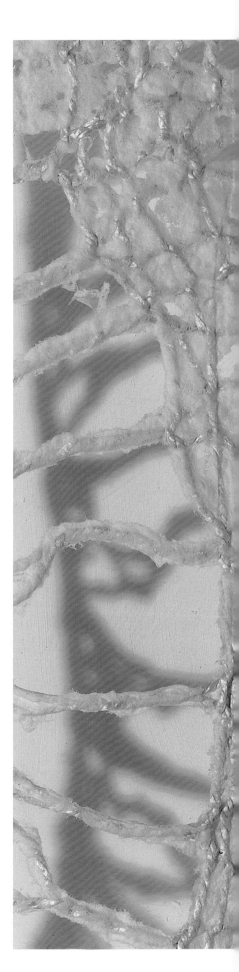

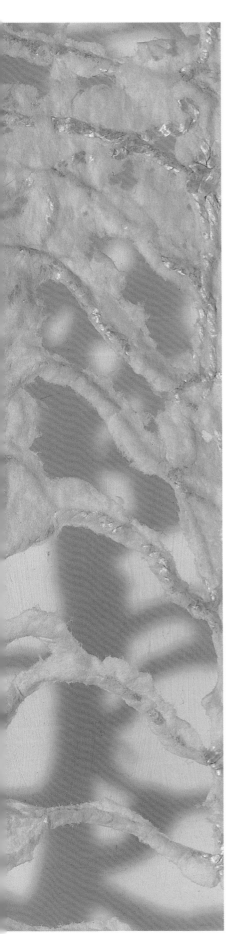

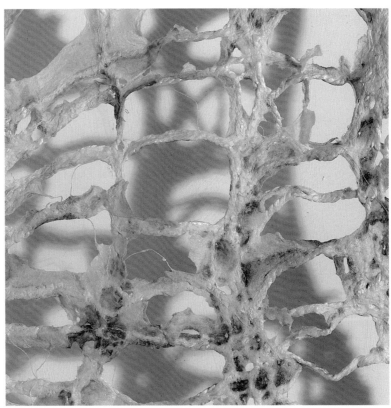

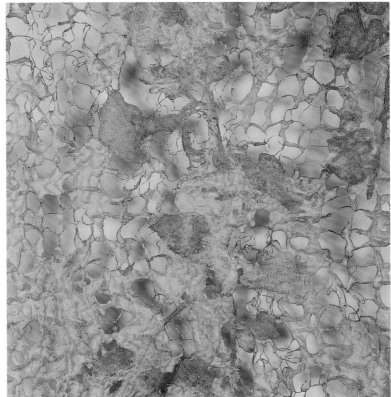

Above: *Knitted wire forms the basis of this piece by Liz Heywood, that celebrates the way in which plant forms break down and decay. Paper pulp enriches the structure that is further embellished with hand and machine stitching.*

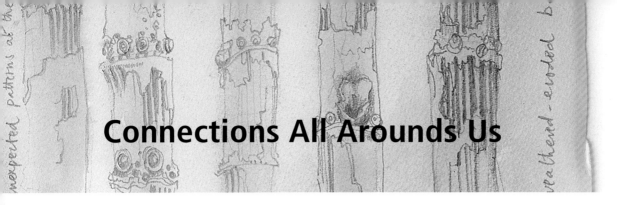

Connections All Arounds Us

Surfaces, objects and people all connect to something or somebody. They can be joined physically and emotionally while others visually appear to be connected by their particular placement.

By selecting and focusing on such a theme, your eyes will become attuned and you will make surprising discoveries. Remember that learning to really look encourages you to see rather than what you think you can see. Develop a visual curiosity and jot down general observations. The more you look the more you will find to inspire and stimulate your awareness of colour, texture and pattern. Ideas for creating designs using connecting lines and shapes can be seen all around us in every day life.

Your own house and garden could reveal many design starting points. Rows of vegetables, seed pods, complex veining within leaves and overlapping profusions of stems and flowers are always appealing. Garden centres display a great assortment of connecting produce. Trays of plastic pots with flowers growing abundantly and entwining with others may well suggest a repeating pattern of networks. Racks of trailing plants or rows of hanging baskets could be simply interpreted into formal or asymmetrical patterns. Climbing plants and their supporting structures offer other considerations.

Even the fencing section could inspire. Lengths of bamboo intricately lashed together, diagonal trellis, various forms of 'woven' wicker and wrought iron fencing incorporating scrolls and pinnacles could suggest other design developments.

An assortment of wire meshes designed for ground cover, plant protection or supports are available in a range of sizes and grids. They could be used as a

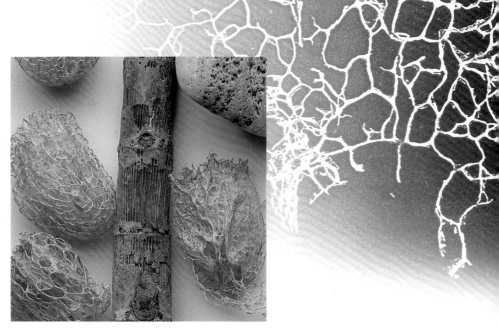

background and provide an exciting alternative network to suspend, wrap, distort, stitch or darn other materials and images during the creative process. Even a train journey can reveal fascinating observations such as bridge structures, sections from cranes, wrought iron supports to roofs, platform tiles and many other features.

By making fast sketches, even when the train is moving, will necessitate a swift reaction to select the main shapes only and will preclude any unnecessary detailing. Quick jottings will not only increase your observation skills but your confidence too. Keep your sketchbook or notebook as a private diary until you feel more sure of yourself. (see Book 12 A Sketch in Time)

Left Page: *This page from a sketchbook shows pencil and wash studies of a dried out length of bamboo found on a beach in Greece. The general textured surface first appealed but further investigation using a magnifying glass revealed fascinating shapes and markings at each section join. Certain elements were taken out of context and stylised drawings were developed from the initial sketches. These in turn inspired the machine embroidered trials worked on soluble fabric. This approach would be suitable for the decoration of garments and fashion accessories.*

This Page: *Worked by machine stitching on soluble fabric, this network was inspired by unravelling the seedpod (see above). The photocopies helped to simplify the complex structure. Two lines of straight stitches were machined one on another before a tiny (1.5 width) zigzag stitch was sewn on top to strengthen and retain the shape firmly. Remember that when machining zigzag stitch on soluble cloth it must be worked on top of a straight stitch otherwise it will unravel when the back ground cloth is washed away.*

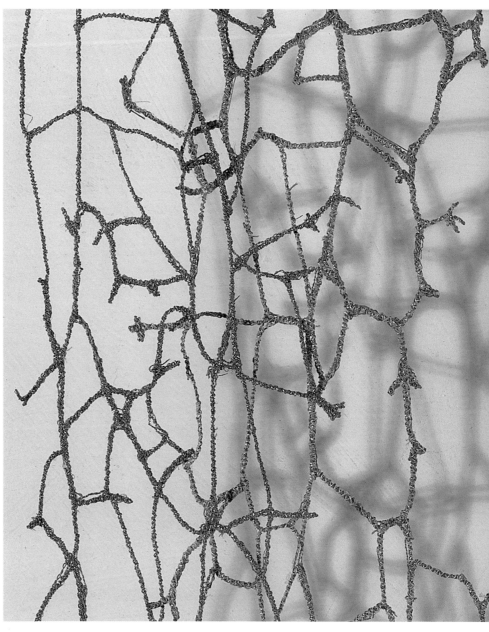

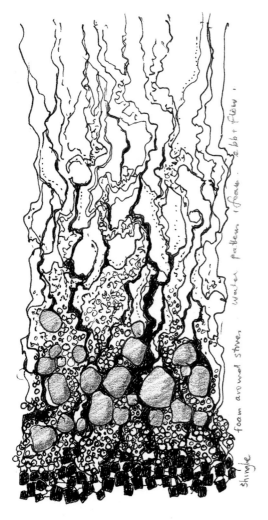

foam around stone   water pattern (foam : ebb + flow).

shingle

Seaside Connections

Being by the sea can provide extensive opportunities for broadening your collection of ideas where connections and networks are the primary themes.

The connecting lines between the sky, sea and land can offer so many variations just by observing the changing weather conditions. Rough, turbulent seas will set up certain rhythms progressing to a stronger ebb and flow where it swirls and pounds the shoreline with more spray, froth bubbles and consequently a greater drag movement of sand and stones. On a still day the crystal clear sea will exhibit gentle ripples where the water meanders quietly around the stones at the waters edge.

Wave patterns and shadowy reflections are extremely hard to capture in a drawing as they are ever changing and distorting into new rhythms and arrangements. Some of the knitting networks can capture the essence quite successfully. (see page 12/13)

Sand patterns found on land after a retreating tide or seen under water when swimming or snorkelling are very beautiful in their simplicity. Again the movement of the water fashions the surface and chisels patterns some of which are slightly indicated or deeply grooved.

The motions of tides and currents show their power with the under water plant life or their debris and these can be cast into amazing entangled networks of patterns. Algae and parasites sometimes add colour and contrasting elements.

Writing down descriptions can be beneficial. One observation made recently was noted as follows.

'The early morning sun is shining obliquely on the tiny wet stones at the shoreline and momentarily changing the colours to sparkling, dancing silvers and soft pearlised colours. Design wise the tonal change of the beige and grey stones may help to integrate the colours of the sparkling water lapping at the waters edge. Gentle water patterns and their reflective qualities seem at one with the pebbles.'

Many of these selected observations could be simplified, exaggerated, stylised into intriguing networks that could lead to numerous textile interpretations.

Top Left: *Stylised design suggested by water patterns and froth bubbles flowing around stones.*

Middle Left: *The asymmetrical pattern was taken from an eroded section of a stone.*

Bottom Left: *Sketch of underwater plant life - aquarelle crayons and pencils.*

This bold dimensional arrangement was initially suggested by a set of under water sketches. The pink and orange algae featured brightly and was a surprising observation. These elements were chosen to be exaggerated. The network was machined in a grid format on soluble fabric. These were then hand stitched in straight and backstitches using fine wools. Machine stitches were worked on top to firm and strengthen. The ground cloth was washed away to leave the stucture. A delicate network of translucent beads added contrast.

Connecting Landscapes

Viewing landscape from the air underlines the fabulous range of divisions and networks that make up the surface of the earth. Fields or prairies that spread for miles have roads, tracks or irrigation channels to divide and sub divide them. These areas contrast with the haphazard arrangement of 'patchwork' fields, their connecting elements being ditches, hedgerows or fences.

Rivers and their tributaries demonstrate other linear networks. They flow through flat plains or chiselled, dimensional mountainous areas, each offering such different characteristics to develop. Seen from the sky, acres of formal rows of olive trees make wondrous patterns of connecting dots, as do the blue green shrubs that are so prevalent in Australia.

Closer observations reveal dividing borders, hedgerows and fences each with there own characteristics that can be high lighted. Hedgerows that contain a range of shrubs and small trees, which have been encouraged to grow and entwine with the each other, create a continuous barrier or division of farmland.

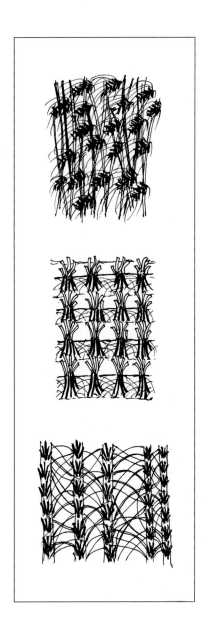

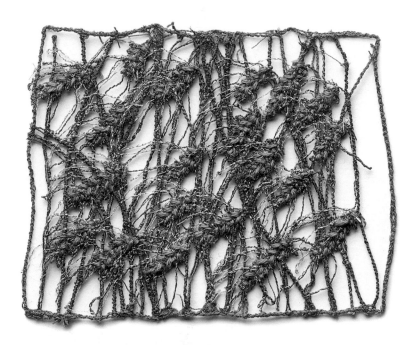

Wire mesh fences forming a diamond lattice framework can provide an interesting foil for integrating applied stitched imagery of wild flowers, grasses or vegetation. Alternatively, it could be the connecting device for a simple colour statement of land and sky.

Crops growing in a field are cultivated in lines and grid formations and present an overall network of patterns. Within that arrangement fully-grown produce can interconnect within the basic formation. Looking through, under or down through the foliage will suggest further views and choices.
All these starting points and dozens of others that you will discover can be simplified, stylised or abstracted to inspire unusual joins and connections.

The sketch (above left) shows a harvested cornfield where the stubble contrasted with the flattened stalks between the lines. The low afternoon sun casts strong shadow patterns as well as adding silvery highlights. The simplified, stylised drawings (far left) were contrived into interconnecting patterns.

The two trial samples were machine stitched onto soluble fabric. Hand stitches were added before being machined again to integrate the two elements (see Book 9). The trials were attempted in order for decisions to be made regarding thickness of line and to ensure that all areas were connected properly. Further work could iron out any structural problems and allow refinements to be added.

An oil seed rape field, where the remaining stalks had been bleached by the sun (see sketch above) inspired the designs on this page. Card and paper collages help to simplify the imagery. Fine networks of machine stitching underpin the sample shown before applied felts and hand stitches developed the surface further.

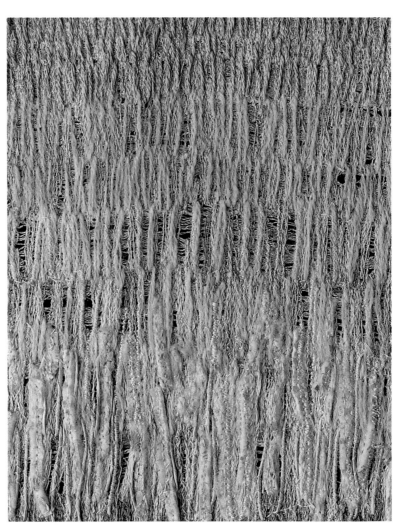

Trees and bushes seen on the top of hills where they appear to meet the sky could provide another design challenge.

Modified to fit a design brief they could form an interesting connecting border demonstrating a balanced but irregular pattern. Certain elements that particularly appeal can be repeated, rotated, distorted or arranged haphazardly depending on the overall aim for the piece to be made. Always allow time to make thumbnail sketches in order to review varying compositions to extend your options.

The suggestions illustrated could be suitable plans for panels, quilts or hangings where the connecting elements are within the design. Patchwork, quilting, appliqué, machine and hand stitching could all be selected.

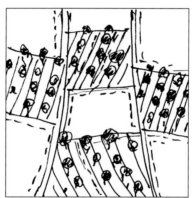

Creating an exciting fragile open work piece could present a further challenge although a few extra connecting lines may have to be added to stabilise the piece. This application may well capture the essence of the place without the conflict of a literal interpretation.

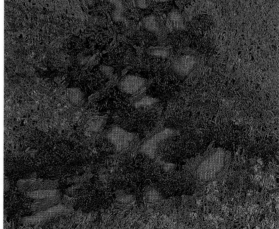

1: Quick sketches drawn with a pen while travelling back to the airport by coach through mountainous Greek landscape. There was only time to jot down a few lines and accompanying notes. The landscape had been observed during the incoming journey so an aim had been formulated.

2: Four thumbnail sketches of varying arrangements suggesting connecting or joining elements.

3, 4 & 5: The three interpretations shown were worked by machine stitching the designs on soluble fabric so that the olive groves were exaggerated to form the open work connections. This type of landscape always appeals due to the contrasts of rough, rugged elements alongside orderly and elegant aspects. However the focus on the theme, connections and networks, influenced the final choice of emphasis and placements.

In Conclusion

It is hoped that by focusing on specific themes of connections, joins and networks some of the suggestions made in this book will encourage and greatly influence lateral thinking. A number of technical and design possibilities will immerge.

Historical, cultural and traditional aspects are always fascinating to study and can continue to influence design developments. Experimentation is strongly recommended in order to develop knowledge of the technique as well as allowing time to formulate the many ideas that will come to mind.

Numerous textile artists and embroiderers have the love of the subject as a strong connecting force. The same focus could be interpreted as an emotional response both to a chosen subject as well as the actual response of working with fabric and thread.

Creating textiles can reflect a variety of moods and emotions, for instance people standing in a queue waiting for a happy event will display their body shapes overlapping by animated, lively connecting lines. In contrast, a line of refugees may well huddle together and appear to be still and disconsolate: the connecting lines may well reflect this mood. Alternatively, lines of lettering could be incorporated within a network to convey a mood or message.

BJ Adams, the American textile artist chose 'Connecting' as a title for a substantial work. (see detail opposite) Her statement reads, "From the beginning of marks on cave walls, through drawing symbols to create words, to the forming of letters for alphabets, to printed books, the inherent differences, in people and their diverse languages, have hindered communication. We have the opportunity to connect in non-verbal ways."

Physical, technical and conceptual interpretations could well be considered in producing innovative textiles. Concentrating on the themes suggested may inspire you to travel down other creative pathways.

Acknowledgements

Special thanks go to our husbands Philip Littlejohn and Steve Udall, to B.J. Adams, our photographer Michael Wicks and designer Jason Horsburgh for all their help and continuing support. We appreciate very much our former students who have kindly allowed us to show their work.

Further Reading

Prehistoric Textiles - E.J.W. Barber.
Tombs, Graves & Mummies - Editor Paul G. Bahn.
Cloth and Human Experience - Edited by Annette B-Werner & Jane Schneider.
Earth from Above - Yan Arthurs-Bertrand.
The Elements of Design - Rediscovering colours, textures, form and shape - Loan Oei & Cecile De Kegel, Thames & Hudson.
By Nature's Design - Chronicle books, San Francisco.

Double Trouble

Booklets in this series include:

This detail of a beautiful scarf was made by Cindy Kearney. Inspired by birds feathers, a length of knitting was stretched between soluble fabric and machine stitched to stabilise and decorate.

Top: 'Connecting' (detail) by B.J. Adams. Machine embroidered hands on painted swag over a fabric collage of multilingual text. Photo: PRS Associates

Bottom: 'Harbour Lights' (detail) This innovative and exciting piece was created by Mary Klinger by knitting and knotting fishing line and incorporating shards of plastic in the process.

0954601432

Published by
Double Trouble Enterprises.
PO Box 348, Maidenhead,
Berkshire SL6 6XB.
fax: +44(0) 1628 675699
www.doubletrouble-ent.com
Booklet designed by
Jason Horsburgh.
Printed by Gemini Press Ltd.
ISBN No. 0-9546014-3-2

double trouble
enterprises

Over the Line

Couching Rediscovered
By Jan Beaney & Jean Littlejohn

Book - 16

Contents